DOING IT *Scared*

AN INSPIRATIONAL GUIDEBOOK TO FACING AND CONQUERING FEAR

erika bryant

DOING IT SCARED

By

erika bryant

First Printing 2021
Chapter 8 Publishing
ISBN 13: 978-1-7364734-9-8

Author: erika bryant | IG: ebryant22 | erika-bryant.com
Cover Photography By: Shot by Sham Photography | IG: @shotbysham
Hair By: IG: @teresagraydontplay |
Makeup By: IG @nicholerayartistry
Graphic Design by: Verbal Slick | IG: @verbalslick

Forever thankful for the mountains of fear that were reduced to dust beneath my faithful feet. ~eb

This outpouring is dedicated to the God given Tree of Love that grounds me. Rooted in the strength of my dearly departed grandmother Lillie, supported by the branches of my loving mother, encouraging father, and protective big brother alongside extended family and "framily" who have championed me over the years. Wonderfully, decorated by the leaves of my very best friend, god-sister, my brilliant goddess tribe, and exquisitely adorned by the fruit of my hero and life love, Chief. This tree of love is ultimately graced by the sunshine of my incomparable ancestors to whom I'm forever thankful.

Beyond what we wish, and fear may happen
We have another life,
As free and clear as a mountain stream.
-Rumi

TABLE OF CONTENTS

FOREWORD

Hollywood is a place like any other, it has roads, buildings, stores, and people. However, in Hollywood unlike anywhere else in the world, one's impossible and outlandish dreams can eventually become a tangible reality – skyrocketing them into the ethos of superstardom.

With that in mind, fear is hindering and non-discriminating, an obfuscator, cloaking the truth in a blanket of chaos and static noise compelling us to adapt. But if all we seek to do is to adapt and surrender to fear, we may not find ourselves with the changes that we want in our lives. In Doing it Scared, erika intertwines her experience journeying to and through Hollywood, with her first-hand awareness and acknowledgement of fear, while illustrating some ways people can work around (and with) said fears to propel them forward. With her diverse background and refreshing perspective, reading this book may substantively change your relationship with fear forever. erika has managed to gracefully and successfully navigate this space. It is my belief that she can help you to navigate it as well.

~Dr. Allycin Powell-Hicks

Ph.D. – Mental Health Expert / Brand Architect

INTRODUCTION

Fear is one of the most powerful emotions we experience as humans. Although it's been said that FEAR is the acronym of *false evidence appearing real*, while in the grips of it, the strongest, richest, most beautiful or most powerful individual can fall prey to its debilitating hold. There's fear of failure, fear of success, fear of love, fear of being alone, fear of leaving, fear of trying, fear of rejection, fear of allowing one's voice to be heard, and beyond. The list is literally endless. But let's be honest, although it's called FEAR, false evidence appearing real, fear is downright the proverbial boogeyman that we can't fathom ourselves facing at the end of the day. So, with that said the aim here is not to convince you that fear is not real, because it absolutely 1,000 percent is real, but more than that, it's something to conquer and move through and dare I say, a blessing in disguise.

Let's try something: sit for a moment and close your eyes. Imagine fear being an enormous mountain that is so tall you can't see beyond it. It's large, looming and intimidating. It's so large, in fact, that you can't even see its shadow; however, your shadow is reflected upon it. You've been given the task to climb or conquer this mountain. You are a novice at climbing, to say the least, and you don't appear to have the proper instruments to achieve the goal safely. However, you have something inside that nudges you forward, because who doesn't like a challenge? As you begin to climb this mountain, the fear of falling and failing rings loudly in your ears. Something within urges you to turn around, telling you it's not worth the anxiety. You continue forward anyway. Distractions come while on this journey as well as naysayers who also don't believe you belong here climbing this mountain. You continue forward. As you make your way to the mountain's peak, you begin to feel a stronger more assured sense of self. And in the glorious moment that you reach that mountain's peak, you are astonished to see a sea of good things (what I like to call blessings) awaiting your arrival. Pure bliss coupled with exhaustion and relief pours over you. You've made it. You, my friend, have done it. You've conquered your fear!

The intention of painting a picture as simplistic as this is to provide a different perspective when approaching your fears. On this journey of conquering fears, you will have to adopt a new warrior-like mentality that will serve you even on your worst day. Fears are meant to be acknowledged, assessed and then subsequently conquered. The challenge is to travel through the fear because as you move along, the fear falls away like shedding old skin. All in all, in this life, like flowers, if you are not growing, you are dying. Conquering fears is a watering that feeds the soil in which you are planted. It never ends—that is, until you've returned completely to the spirit realm.

Why, you may ask, would or, better yet, should anyone ever want to conquer their fears? Well, as humans our very existence and purpose in this life are expansion. We are meant to expand the meaning of life through our visions, dreams, experiences, journeys, and adventures. As interconnected as we are, we as a collective make life sweeter as the minutes, days and years tick by. We've created and manifested more and more since the beginning of time, and a large part of that was doing something that has never been done before. From creating electricity to something as simple as peanut butter, someone took a risk or followed a dream or inspiration to step outside of the box to do a new thing. If they could do it back then with all of their limitations, why, I ask, can't you? I argue that you, in fact, can and prayerfully will stretch yourself into new directions and areas once you have completed this book.

As you journey with me, I'll share in this motivational handbook moments of fear that I personally experienced and overcame with courage, determination and gentleness. I had to move forward in my own time and at my own pace to truly stand in my truth and become fearless.

In all honesty this book is my attempt at putting to rest a ten-year-old fear that has rested upon my heart quietly yet consistently for as long as I can remember. Being coined the guru of my girlfriends since forever, I've been a sounding board, voice of reason and angel on many shoulders over the years. Humbled and honored by these women who've shared their innermost thoughts, feelings and experiences has been a privilege that I cherish. If my couch could talk it would tell a multitude of colorful stories shared by my lady loves going through family issues, breakups, divorces, depression, anxiety, loss of control, powerlessness, defeat, triumph, abuse, career changes, bankruptcy, cheating, being cheated on, etc. And after each of those encounters the begging question that has always haunted me for days after they've left my home is, "When are you going to write a book? I'd totally buy it." I've said too many times to count, "I'm waiting for the right time," or, "I don't know what to write about."

I had to sit alone in my meditation time to come to the realization that I've been afraid. Afraid of failing. Afraid of no one caring enough to read what I have to say. Afraid of not being successful enough to earn the right to publish a book. Afraid of thinking too much of myself. Afraid of needing the validation of others to shore me up so that I feel worthy enough to write a book. I'm no Deepak or Oprah, how dare I? But here I am, DOING IT SCARED.

Today I'm climbing my mountain as I sit during a national quarantine and pandemic writing my first child. The world has actually stopped, and now I have nothing else distracting me, calling on me, needing me or deterring me. I can't run any longer. More than me writing this book, this book is writing me. It's been in the ethos incubating for quite some time. On the other side of this scary mountain awaits a whole new world.

This outpouring is an expression set with intentions to uplift, inspire and empower people of all ages. When we have the courage to conquer our fears, our life's purpose magically unfolds beneath our very feet. The faith that is required for each subsequent step is somehow innate within us as life continues to call us forward. Trust that anything the mind's eye can see, the universe is not only able but also willing to manifest. And so it is.

While some might suggest that fear is beneath us and that there is some magical spell that will preclude one from ever succumbing to fear, this book will embrace the reality that to fear is to be human. While on this human journey, we cannot escape expansion and growth, which in and of itself promotes a sense of fear as we move toward some new unknown. Does this sound familiar? What are you running from? What are you afraid to do? What are you afraid to conquer? What have you been putting off for another day? Life is not about the destination, but rather the incremental journey that unfolds along the way. From a bird's-eye view, fears are mere speed bumps along that journey.

In essence, fear is our teacher–friend. Yes, fear is a friend. Our annoying teacher– friend that calls us to the carpet and holds us accountable. A friend in the sense that it stretches us into directions unknown and invites us to grow in areas that are beneficial. A teacher in the sense that it is patient and will hold steady, even until death if we allow it. Fear is indeed the protagonist and gateway that propels us toward our destiny. We are meant to travel through fear in order to defeat it—and not cower at its feet. Together, let's DO IT SCARED.

Note: Please Consider having a pen and paper handy while on this journey as we have some important work to do together. There are note pages provided in the rear of the book for convenience.

CHAPTER ONE

DOING IT SCARED BECAUSE

FEAR IS A MOTIVATOR

It's amazing to sit and watch birds of the air or animals in the wild. Have you noticed how confident and fearless they are? They don't have a care in the world. They face danger at every single turn, and they seem to embrace it in a way that is so admirable. They don't question their position or worthiness or worry about what the other animals will think of them. They walk to a rhythm that is their own. Not only that, but also they live in a perpetual *now* that allows them to dwell in bliss— unbothered.

Unlike animals, because of logic, we as the human species are flooded with thoughts of doubt and fear at almost every turn. Our brains remind us of how something played out in the past, causing us to proceed with caution. Wouldn't it be nice to operate like animals do intrinsically? How freeing that would be. However, since that is not the case, we ought to consider using fear to galvanize us. Harnessing it as fuel to propel us toward the life that we want instead of it playing out as perpetual highlight reel of what has gone wrong. In doing so, we must look ahead in life and not allow the past to dictate our future. Much like when driving a car, the windshield provides us with the clearest perception of what's on the road ahead and gets us to our desired destinations, not fixating on what lies behind us in our review mirrors.

My mother has always told me that I was the easiest kid to care for. I'm told I never really cried unless my handsome older brother made me—as he loved to hear me scream as a kid. I remember being conscientious in school and really thriving and excelling off the praise of others. I became a bit of a people pleaser, and oddly, amidst all the drama, I grew to be an eternal optimist—always seeing the brighter side of things. This is something that has feathered my mental nest over the years. My homelife was a troubled one from a child's point of view, riddled with domestic abuse, drugs, gambling and the like. I saw many things that no kid should witness, but I learned to delineate the things I wanted from the things I did not want. The contrasting elements allowed me to observe and choose early on who I could become.

Growing up in an environment that is challenging might make one feel like they are destined for a particularly unfavorable outcome. However, contrast can also present a beautiful opportunity for growth and expansion. As a child the first impressions we have about life come from the adults who surround us. In a substantial number of cases, the adults are a colorful cast of characters who by no fault of their own have strayed from their path and remain stagnant. Their lives seem to have been going along and at one point came to a screeching halt. Since that point it seems that they've remained in a perpetual *Groundhog Day* experience. A child witnessing such a thing may start to believe that this is as good as it gets, that these grownups have all the answers and are following a particular blueprint on which a child can rely. As a child, I quickly learned that this game of life is defined by each player, not by predetermined rules set forth by earlier participants—related or not.

I've always said that if our destinies were predetermined by the experiences of our earlier lives, that in my case, I should have been a drug addict, a criminal or dead by now. Being raised by my father in a single-parent home after he and my mother's domestic issues forced her to abandon my brother and I, was the least of my worries. However, seeing family members who were in and out of jail, doing drugs, dealing drugs, gambling, pimping, prostituting, experiencing house raids and police questioning was a lot to take in. It's a miracle that I chose a different path but only because I was exposed to what I did not want. I was no better than any of them, but I felt (even as a child) my destiny had another trajectory.

Leaving home for college was something that I honestly hadn't thought much about until my senior year of high school. Nobody in my family had attended a four-year college. Even though I was subconsciously setting myself up to pursue a college career, I was quite ambivalent about it initially. Ambivalent because even though my circumstances at home weren't ideal, I couldn't quite envision what life outside of that would look like. With all of the happenings surrounding me, I knew deep down that education would be my golden ticket. I just had no clue what I wanted to do with the ticket once I had it within my grasp.

In school, I'd been a model student. I was on the high honor roll, in the prestigious Touch of Class Choir under the direction of Gregory Cole (*who was like a bonus dad to us*), vice president of my class, and pretty popular among the nerds and the cool kids. I was friends with the teachers, the principal, my guidance counselor and the dean. I'm not sure why I was such a goody two-shoes. I think I felt like there was someone keeping score of all my good deeds. Maybe one day I'd be rewarded for stomaching so much as a kid by life cutting me a break. At any rate I knew deep down that my ticket out of a life that I refused to become a victim to was hidden in me excelling in school. A part of me wanted to spread my wings and take flight across the country to see what life might show me. What if every dream I ever had hinged on me leaving to achieve it? What if staying home was truly the trap that I'd often convinced myself it was. Hell, I'd seen no one leave and return to tell about it. But what did I have to lose? To be clear, staying home and watering my roots there would not have been the end of me, but I certainly would not be living the life I have today. I'd be a different version of myself,

I'm certain.

Like anyone, home was my comfort zone no matter how dysfunctional. I found comfort in dancing with the devil I knew. The devil I didn't know is what scared me. The what-ifs kicked in: What if I got to college and couldn't handle the workload? What if at the first taste of freedom I'd run wild and get distracted from school? The what-ifs will taunt us and paint pictures in our mind's eye that cause us to forfeit or abort our dreams before they can even take root.

We had no money for me to attend school, so what would happen after my initial grant money for my first semester was gone? What would I do? My mom was afraid for me to attend college out of state, which I'm certain was based on her own fears. What if her fears were right? What did I know? I was seventeen years old.

I could not answer any of those haunting questions, but what I did know is that the fear of going away to college slowly diminished as the fear of not going increased. It's funny how the universe will meet you right where you are, lend you exactly what you need, and speak it in a language that is easily digestible. I remember going to speak with a college prep counselor on several occasions as she was guiding me through my college application process. When I expressed my fears about going out of state, she softly reminded me that home would always be there. So if leaving forever was too big of a pill to swallow at the time, I could tell myself that I was just going to try it on for size. For some odd reason that clicked into place for me and I was able to allow the anxiety that was causing me so much internal strife to subside.

Deep down I knew that once I left home I'd never return, but I was too inexperienced in life to make a life choice at that time. Or so I thought.

Have you ever been in a place where comfort turned to complacency? Are you there now? Have you ever allowed the fears of others dictate your course of action? Has the upset of remaining the same become so stale that you've blamed yourself for not climbing your mountain? Fear disguised as mountains comes in all shapes and forms: starting a business, traveling, moving, being in a relationship, forgiving a loved one, standing up for oneself, leaving a relationship, keeping one's integrity in the face of others, having children, getting married, deciding not to have children, getting out of debt, etc. Our goal should be to acknowledge when we are scared and accept it. Allow the fear to exist and embrace it. Then, over time, the goal is to softly release our resistance through answering revealing questions so we can soothe ourselves into a place of freedom beyond that fear.

DOING IT SCARED

What are some mountains you have chosen not to climb? Remembering that we *always* have a choice, acknowledge that there may have been some deeper fears associated with those choices. As an exercise, write down on a piece of paper three mountains (fears) that you have been too afraid to climb—places where fear may have gotten the best of you in a particular situation. Maybe you simply have chosen to ignore or have refused to climb these mountains. After listing them, explore the reasons why you chose those paths. How would your life potentially be different had you climbed those mountains?

TAKEAWAYS:

- Contrast can also present a beautiful

opportunity for growth and expansion.

- The what-ifs will taunt us and paint pictures in our mind's eye that cause us to forfeit or abort our dreams before they can even take root.

- Allow the fear to exist and embrace it, because over time the goal is to softly release our resistance through answering revealing questions, so we can soothe ourselves into a place of freedom beyond it.

CHAPTER TWO

DOING IT SCARED BECAUSE

NO MATTER WHAT YOU'RE FACING

YOU CAN MANIFEST ANYTHING

Childbirth is one of life's most miraculous and magical occurrences. It's a woman sacrificing her body as she lends it as a portal for life itself to manifest. It's a naturally selfless and magical phenomenon that is quite baffling when you think about it. The body knows exactly what to do and almost goes into an autopilot mode when in labor.

The breath is essential in the process because it carries life and aligns the mother with the child as it's guided through her womb. In sync, two souls dance for hours through the laboring process finding a rhythm that bonds them for eternity. Both of their worlds are upon the precipice of change. The embryo has lived a life in water since inception and has been protected inside a sacred bubble. Not impervious to the ills and stresses taken on by the mother, he or she rests insulated safely in the belly. Not yet a mother myself, I marvel at those who have been chosen by little sprits to host them in this life journey. I've witnessed how friends embarking upon such an adventure are riddled with feelings of fear, honor, joy, worry and anxiety, to name a few.

It's quite profound to sit and watch as newborns transform into infants, then toddlers, and beyond. The first several months of their budding lives are so critical as they begin to hold up their heads, roll over, crawl and eventually walk. It would be interesting to know what a child who's learning to walk is thinking as they are taking literal baby steps. It's a lot to consider with gravity, balance, the type of flooring, the type of shoe, etc. Considering all things, do they experience fear or anxiety as they walk it out? They are often being encouraged by loved ones who've mastered walking, but is that even a consideration? Do they fear their first steps? Without the gift of words and vocabulary it's unlikely that we'll ever know. But how brave are they for trying and falling, trying and stumbling, trying and barely making it a step before plopping on their cute bottoms? This simple analogy affirms that our inner self calls us forward even at an early age. It truly is up to us to answer the call. I've never seen a toddler who wanted to walk but refused to because of fear or their unwillingness to fall. And you'll notice that after the first step there comes another, and another, and another until they are stepping, then walking, then running. I don't know if babies can see themselves running when they haven't even mastered walking, but that doesn't stop them from taking the first step. It's quite inspiring when you think about it.

Once away at college, I was able to find my footing and ground myself with the help of trusted family and friends who were rooting for my success. The fear of going backward was probably my biggest motivator. It was as if I was dropped in the middle of the ocean and given the option to swim back or swim ahead. Not knowing what may lie ahead, I chose forward motion. This was my first go at living a life untethered and unsupervised. I loved every minute of it. The only picture I'd had of college was from the television show *A Different World*, and my campus at Clark Atlanta University and AU Center had to have been the inspiration behind that creative genius. There were parties, and boys, and drinking, and boys, study groups, and boys, step shows, and boys, pep rallies, and boys, basketball games, and did I mention the boys?

But it wasn't all fun and games. During my schooling I had to get a job in order to support myself, as the financial aid and loans barely covered my tuition each semester. In addition to my job at the mall and picking up an internship at a local up-and-coming music studio, Patchwerk Recordings, I also got another part-time internship at the legendary LaFace Records. I figured staying busy would keep me focused on my studies and out of trouble. And trust me, there was some trouble to get into. I honestly had no clue what I wanted to do after college, but I knew I wanted to enjoy myself and maybe not have a regular nine-to-five. I wanted my life to be more fluid and maybe even be my own boss one day, but oddly it's something I never gave much thought to back then. Maybe my internal method was to wing it so to speak. I knew I wanted to be in the music business but I had no clue what that required or entailed. Atlanta certainly exposed me to entrepreneurship in a way that I never knew was possible, as it was nonexistent as far as I knew prior to that. The only entrepreneurs I knew growing up were hustlers and drug dealers, and although they had a lavish lifestyle, that definitely was not a path I had in mind for myself.

Ultimately destiny called me forward into directions of areas unknown and I was impetuous and naïve enough to journey forward. Believe it or not, fear of failure was also the wind at my back propelling me toward the unknown, for I knew what was behind me and I feared returning there. Interestingly, sometimes knowing what we don't want clarifies and crystalizes exactly what we do want. And at this point I knew I wanted peace of mind, and success which in my mind has always amounted to wealth.

I vividly remember my first day at the iconic LaFace Records, who churned out hits from the likes of Toni Braxton, TLC, Outkast, Goodie Mob, Tony Rich and Usher. I'd interviewed a couple of times hoping to land a coveted spot on their intern roster. I got overlooked on the first pass, but a few months later it was my turn. I was so nervous on my Marta train ride there as I watched the businessmen and women in a zombie-like zone headed toward Buckhead. I had no classes that day because being an eternal overachiever, I liked to book all of my classes on Tuesday and Thursday, so I'd have the alternate days to work and intern. It was no small feat to squeeze in eighteen hours of credits into a two-day school schedule, but I was determined. When I got to the beautiful high-rise glass building, I signed in at security and made my way up toward destiny, or so I thought. I was greeted by the sweetest receptionist at the front desk named Regina, who was also from the Bay Area, and her calm eased my nerves a bit. I felt so out of place and oddly small—a way I hadn't felt since I was a young girl being bullied in elementary school because I was so tiny compared to my classmates. Before I knew it, I was rushing to the bathroom to bless the porcelain gods with my morning breakfast. After collecting myself I got situated, and my new journey began. In the midst of being thrust into this new experience, I learned a lot quickly. Looking back, I couldn't really wrap my head around what was happening and how monumental these moments were, but it didn't matter because this was the beginning. The beginning of what? Well, only God knew the answer to that, but I was happy to exist in this newfound place of self-discovery.

Have you ever begun to climb a mountain or address a fear, and all of the anxiety you anticipated beforehand reared its ugly face? Do you remember what you did in that situation? More likely than not, in the midst of that ordeal you stuck with it and pushed through until the end or completion. Why do you presume that is? Again, there is something about our inner beings that calls us forward into the very things we have been wishing for, imagining or praying about. We are natural-born creators of our life experiences. We manifest whatever we spend any amount of time focusing on. And whatever we focus on the most is what we attract into our lives.

Just as in nature, whatever plants we water are the plants that grow. Adversely, the same plants will shrivel and die without sunlight, love and most importantly, water and attention. What plants have you been watering? What do you spend most of your time thinking about and focusing on? The way to assess the answer to this is to look at the output in your life. If you spend a good amount of time complaining about not trusting people, I guarantee that you have been and will continue to attract untrustworthy people into your life. Or if your common complaint is that there are no good men out there, you tend to attract the men that live up to that standard exactly. But what if you simply changed your expectation? What if you decided to *choose* (there's that word again) a new thought or opinion on any given subject matter? What do you presume would happen? Perhaps it's time we find out.

For example, there are a few friends that I have who are confident, beautiful, smart, funny, and financially stable but they struggle in the area of dating. The conversation is often counterintuitive to they claim to want, which is a good, stable, supportive and emotionally available man. (Of course, the actual lists are as long as my arm, but we'll stop here.) However, instead of seeing and talking about the positives that exists in the guys that they meet, they tend to give more airtime to the negative aspects. How the guys don't call enough, make more of an effort, or claim them as a number one priority. So, year after year they tend to attract the same men—new names, new faces, but same the guys. So I argue , until the expectation and conversation (which is an outpouring of what we believe) around the things we desire change, then the circumstances won't change either. It's time we become newscasters instead of news reporters. Why don't we forecast what we want versus reporting what's right in front of us? Because we enjoy talking about what we see and are experiencing and want the validation of others to affirm that we are being wronged in some way. That's all fine and good, but in the end, we are only shortchanging ourselves and holding ourselves apart from what we already have access to through our words and affirmations. Remember, what we affirm, we confirm. Not the other way around.

We are so immensely gifted as human beings, and God has empowered us to create our very own realities. This principle goes against the notion that our lives are predetermined and that we are merely actors playing a role that we have no influence or say so in. But in the Bible, it speaks of the power of life and death being in the tongue, which is the most lethal weapon we possess. So, if we have the power to speak things into being, "Speak those things that are not as though they were" (Romans 4:17), then that must mean that we have some authority over our lives. Have you ever noticed that the more attention and conversation you lend to something, the more prevalent it becomes? How many times have you spoken against the very thing you've been wanting because your current reality paints a different picture? Or no matter how much you may want something new, the thing that you complain about is what seems to constantly manifest?

Our words are alive—they are life in motion. So, what you place your thoughts, focus and words upon are what you are *choosing* to breathe life into. We get what we expect 100 percent of the time. Our expectations can either benefit us or harm us, elevate us or eliminate us.

So, my friends who are in search of a healthy, loving relationships with stable and caring partners, can have exactly that. What they want is more than possible to obtain, but before those desires can manifest, they have to speak about the situation as if it's already in their midst. As adults it may seem weird to imagine and daydream about our lives and what the future might hold. But trust me, take a step back and look at your life. *You* spoke and imagined your way to this very moment. I'm happy to be here with you, but what's next? What kind of life are you creating for yourself?

What if we allowed ourselves to dream, imagine and *expect* that the magic of the universe is backing us with every step? Does knowing that you have a choice in all that matters to you make you feel empowered at all? Do you even realize how powerful you are? Maybe that power frightens you, but I encourage you again to do it scared.

DOING IT SCARED

What have you been talking about this past week? Recount your conversations with each person and ask yourself how many times you shared a specific story that wasn't necessarily favorable. It could have been about work, your partner, or someone you wish was your partner, a family member, your car, the people at church, your boss, or even your children. No matter the subject, your conversation about it is what you have been watering. It's very sobering to know that we have so much control over our experience, but we are often unknowingly mismanaging it. None of us wants to sabotage our lives and be miserable, yet many of us walk around letting life live us instead of the other way around.

After recounting the conversations, jot down a very brief summary of exactly what happened. Don't spend too much time on this as the goal is not to rehash it – just state it and move on. Beneath that write everything surrounding that scenario that went right. Maybe it was a beautiful day, or someone gave you a much-needed compliment, or your favorite song was played on the radio. Literally sift out anything that was pleasant. Then ask yourself was there anything that was not so bad about the occurrence? Can you find any humor? What did you notice or discover? Be extremely detailed in this version. Point out what you learned from the situation? Did you learn something about you or someone else? How will that new information help you going forward? Did you gain clarity about something? You are essentially attempting to insulate the event with positive reinforcement. Forecasting it differently can shift your thinking and more importantly *(eventually)* your expectation. Abraham Hicks states that, "A belief is just a thought you keep thinking." So, that means it's imperative to shift our thoughts to the things that we desire and want no matter how the situation might appear.

Once our true internal beliefs about something harmonize with our desires – we are able to manifest them. Standing in our power, we envision and then stand in expectation – it's like magic. It might seem lofty, but it is universal law. For example, this week I heard numerous conversations where people were complaining about being quarantined under the stay-at-home order. How they are bored, miss their old lives, and hate that their freedoms to move about are being infringed upon. But I noticed when life was normal, they complained then as well. Another prime example is that of people who constantly complain that they are broke (without money). Because of those persistent words and that constant belief - that is exactly what their experience will forever be - broke. Until they can envision and eventually believe they are wealthy – they'll never attain that desire. And it's important to note that wealth comes in many forms. Wealthy in talent, health, love, family, friendships, laughter and on and on. Choosing to focus on other variations of wealth can eventually impact wealth in currency. Ultimately, we cannot manifest what we don't believe, no matter how strong the desire might be.

Staying mindful of our words and remaining in a place of appreciation and gratitude is critical to living the lives we dream about as well. Once you have cast a more positive light on your chosen conversation, read it through a couple of times and take notice of your internal self-chatter. Is your mind telling you how it actually transpired and not allowing you to reimagine the situation and point out the positives? If this is the case, fret not. It's fine, as this takes a good deal of practice. Awareness is the point to focus on so you can begin to see things as you want them to be. Then with time and consistency, things will begin to shift to look like what you have envisioned.

TAKEAWAYS:

- Sometimes fear helps us to see that life is about knowing what you don't want.

- Our thoughts become our words, which manifest into our actions. We should consider being mindful of our inner dialogue.

- What you talk about expands and you give life to. What are you breathing life into with your words?

CHAPTER THREE

DOING IT SCARED

BECAUSE YOU REALLY CAN FLY!

Fear is a sneaky bugger. It will come at you from all sides using tactics to antagonize, intimidate and discourage you. It will not only play internally on your psyche, but it will present itself in the people that you trust, love and admire the most. Have you ever been forced by external forces to face a fear? Sometimes in our refusal to choose, we are chosen. And our indecision actually becomes the deciding factor.

There was a time when life pushed me forward after working in the music industry for nearly a decade. And I say pushed because I'd become so complacent in my routine that I was deathly afraid of anything else—it was my new normal. I was working at one of the most premier music studios in Atlanta, the now legendary Patchwerk Recordings. I'd literally begun my career there. It was the mid to late '90s in Atlanta when the culture was exploding on the music scene. Outkast, Goodie Mob, TLC, Ludacris, TI, Usher, Attic Crew, Lil John, Bad Boy and a ton of other artists were our regular clients. Atlanta became known as the Black Mecca during this period. Crunk music, Freaknik and booty shake was the order of the day, and we were loving it. I'd never imagined that this would be part of my experience after climbing that mountain and venturing off to college. Here in this time and space, I had the opportunity to create myself as I wanted.

Still very young I had no plan for what I wanted to do long term. Music had always been my heartbeat since I was a small child, instilled in me by my parents, but I had no clue how it would play a part in my life. I honestly sort of fell into this sect of music after applying for an internship. I was on campus at Clark Atlanta University hanging out after a class and noticed a flyer posted near the library. I had been only focused on my studies and not gotten involved in any extracurricular activities after being burned out in high school. Not much outside of school really interested me except for maybe the thought of pledging at some point. I was having too much fun in this new world and didn't want any responsibility outside of studying. Life after my first semester wasn't promised because my scholarship monies were not renewable, so I could be back home within a year's time. At any rate, on this day something made me notice this flyer, so I pulled a tab that listed out the info of who to call, etc. I went in for an interview and met the guys that ran the studio: the owner, Bob, who played for the Atlanta Falcons, and his childhood friends, Curtis and BJ, who he'd built this studio and business with. They, too, hailed from California (Carson), so I felt like it might be a cool place to land for a while. They were like a family, and since I had no roots in Atlanta at the time, here is where God planted me.

The environment in Atlanta at the time was pulsing with a sense that told us we could do and conquer anything. It was as if the air was different, and everyone felt it. To put it plainly, it was magical, and it was a very charmed beginning to my journey.

I spent years there and worked my way up to a managerial position where I was second in command regarding the daily function of the business. I learned a great deal and met so many amazing people who I respect and admire to this day. I spent eight years there. I attended college, graduated college and was still there. It was home, my safe place, but sometimes home can be so comfortable that it tricks us into believing that it's God's best for us. And maybe for a period it was, but that doesn't mean we are to cling to it in fear of the unknown road that might lie ahead.

My employer Curtis became somewhat of a big brother/mentor to me, and he saw my potential eons before I did. To this day I'm unsure of what exactly he honed-in on, but he clearly saw something that I did not. He would softly nudge and encourage me that there were bigger things I could accomplish, but honestly the thought of leaving the only stability I'd had since being a child was not desirable. The people on this job literally became my second family, with whom I spent holidays and experienced various triumphs and pitfalls. For me this was an intricate and layered labyrinth of fears. If I were to leave, what would I do? Yes, I'd graduated from college, but school was all that I really knew I was great at. I had worked at this job for eight years and learned how to manage people. I had emerged as a leader, something I never knew was possible or plausible. So, to say I was comfortable would be an understatement.

However, changes were on the horizon for the company, and there was talk of Cash Money Records potentially buying out the music studio, lock, stock and barrel—or at least this is what I was told, perhaps to nudge me toward my destiny.

It's really profound how God and the universe will prick our hearts when it's something we must do. First, it's a thought, then a whisper, then writing on the wall, a blaring sign, or finally a physical manifestation that is impossible to ignore. I've always been a very determined person, and if ever unclear on what I want, I'm never unclear about what I don't want. For me, the personal aha moment that it might be time to move on or at least to start preparing myself for something new came when I least expected it.

I was working late one day, alone in the office and watching an interview with Oprah Winfrey. I was partly listening as I was working on payroll, when something caught my attention. She was speaking about holding a job that she was no longer enamored by; it had lost its luster. Then what stood out to me was her saying that there is nothing like going to a job every day that you no longer love or lack excitement for because a small piece of you is slowly dying (I'm paraphrasing). We didn't have VTR back then, so I couldn't rewind and play it back for clarity. But the thing is, I didn't need to! I heard her and the sentiment behind what she was saying loud and clear—so much so that tears began to stream down my face because I knew in my heart that it would soon be time to leave this place that I'd called home.

The fear of this notion barreled down on me like a Mack truck. Where would I go? What would I do? Yes, I had a degree in television/radio/film, but practically speaking, my degree didn't compare to having hands-on training like some of my peers were experiencing. I'll be honest, that moment in the office came and then passed. I didn't share it with anyone because even that frightened me. I was in denial and not ready to even explore the possibilities, let alone accept the truth of what I knew was bound to happen. Fast-forward to several months later, and God used the man that had been my mentor to present me with an ultimatum. Either I could stay at the company and be paid half of my salary, or I could take a small severance and leave the company. It's funny how God will use those closest to us. They look like bullies, and sometimes they are. Some bullies come to hold you back, and others come to push you forward. In this instance he was the latter. I, of course, could not see that at the time. I felt abandoned, betrayed and angry. After a three-day fast, I decided it was best for me to leave. Thinking back, I believe even me praying and fasting was rooted in fear, and perhaps was a stall tactic in hopes that God would change his mind. It was me saying, "God, are you sure? Maybe HE needs to see the error in his ways and reconsider this!" It's pretty hilarious, honestly.

Hindsight is twenty-twenty, and it's clear to me now that my wings were fully developed, trained and nurtured. It was time for me to trust in my own wings to fly. I'll be honest, today I am eternally grateful for Curtis' gentle nudge that I perceived as an aggressive shove. When initially attempting to fly solo, that first step out of the nest can be a doozy. You actually free-fall a bit before the flying part kicks in. At least this was my experience. I actually felt like I was nose-diving toward the concrete before my wings initiated. That might sound a bit dramatic, but at the time so many things had fallen apart, and that's exactly how I felt. My constant self-talk was, "I lost my job (when I actually chose to leave), my boyfriend cheated and then dumped me, and now I might lose both houses I worked so hard to get." It was a lot for my twenty-six-year-old self to grapple with. As my mom would often say, when it rains, it pours. And if this was adulting, I hated it!

I was forced to climb a mountain that I'd been avoiding. Destiny was pulling me forward—and I eventually went, kicking and screaming. Sound familiar at all? Can you recount a time when you resisted some inevitability? Stuck in a place, you stood paralyzed in the face of the unknown? In an effort to remain in and maintain some version of control, you refused to move or change? Looking back now with the gift of hindsight, that was one of the best decisions I've ever made in my adult life.

Ultimately, I very well could have stayed at that job, taken the pay cut and continued to let life live me instead of the other way around. Instead, I not only left that job, but I changed my focus completely. The degree I'd earned was about to be put to work, and that previous chapter was slowly coming to a close. It was time to take a leap of faith and bet on myself. Friends, we were not only meant to fly, but to soar! The fears that we adopt threaten the very essence of who we're born to be. I know now for certain that when I feel fear creeping into the back door of my mind, I must address it. And not only address it, but if I feel a strong resistance to moving forward from that spot, that is a clear signal that I *must* walk directly toward it and rip it off like a Band-Aid. I have loathed these moments in the past, but now that I understand that fear is my teacher, I'm encouraged that beyond the shadow of fear is a new level for me.

Have you ever bet on yourself? It's one of the most fulfilling and rewarding feelings, because it's a sure thing! What area of your life have you been choosing to stand still in? Knowing that there is an alternative to the narrative, what holds you back?

DOING IT SCARED

Sometimes when facing a fear, it's important to really unpack what is going on and allow our minds to venture there. A writing technique that I like to employ centers around allowing just that. It's the *what-if . . . game*. Begin by writing something that you have been wanting to do in your life, but due to circumstance, you have yet to take the first step. Maybe it's starting a business, or moving, or like me, changing careers. Under that subject make a list of what-if questions that flood your mind surrounding the subject, leaving space to address the question later. Once you do that, then go back to each what-if statement and think about how it could potentially play out if what you wrote were to come true. The point of this is to prove that we often think of the worst outcome, but when we really look at a matter from a rational standpoint, we can dispel the myths that we've built around our fears.

TAKEAWAYS:

- The fears that we adopt threaten the very essence of who we're born to be.

- There is an internal answer for every life question that poses itself. We just have to quiet ourselves and be still for a moment to hear

- Prayer works!

- YOU CAN FLY! Whatever that means to you regarding answering the call of destiny, you were made especially for this life and your calling.

- Don't wait for people to bet on you. Bet on yourself!

CHAPTER FOUR

DOING IT SCARED BECAUSE

FEAR IS A MIRROR OF ILLUSIONS

HOPE IS THE BRIDGE BETWEEN LOVE AND FEAR

Perfect love casts out fear. —I John 4:18

It is my belief that love is the antithesis of fear. Or better stated, love is fear's antidote. Love is the kryptonite that cripples fear, bringing it to its very knees. Fear crumbles in the face of love. And by love, I mean the self-care, nourishment and appreciation that we are exactly where we need to be at any given moment, and that place is alright. It's all right and it's alright. Love is so many things because it's subjective, as it varies from person to person and subject to subject. It's impossible to define, as it is infinite in its existence and expansion. But it's pure magic in the face of fear. And we all can tap into love at will because it's something we were all born with. All people are created the same in that one vertical of love granted to us by God at creation. But how does one travel from a place of fear to a place of love to move forward?

In the classic *The Wizard of Oz*, the characters overcame their fears by tapping into what was already within them. They had to dig deep, connect with their inner beings, and experience varied circumstances to motivate them toward their individual and collective destinies. Love was the courage of the Lion, the heart of the Tin Man, and the brain of the Scarecrow. It was Dorothy's shoes! While on that yellow brick road journey, they each had moments when they internally and outwardly pledged to give up or throw in the towel. They wanted to be left alone and lay complacent in their version of normal. Initially, the pain of moving ahead in whatever fear was plaguing them was far too big of a burden to bear. But with each other's help and encouragement, they began to believe more in themselves than before. Eventually, they began to trust, just a little, that maybe they could be more. Maybe they could do more. Maybe they could achieve what others had, go places others went and return home to the truth of who they were born to be. Just maybe. Maybe they could indeed live the life they'd always dreamed of. And eventually, they each did. There is such a beautiful sentiment in this classic tale that encourages us to be a witness to our fears and then love ourselves through the pain of forging ahead and doing it scared anyway.

A NEW PERSPECTIVE

I'm sure that many have not looked at love through this particular lens before, but it's something worth considering.

Fear is mighty, but love is the powerful magic that aligns and calibrates us to hear the call of destiny. Love shakes us from complacency when it causes us to say to ourselves, "Why them and not me?" "Could I ever do that?" "Could that ever be me?" "When will it be my turn?" Or statements like, "I wish that were me." Or, "I hope that's me one day."

Or, "They are so lucky." For some reason we tend to see ourselves as grasshoppers instead of the giants we were born to be. Those people that are doing "that thing" have merely tapped into their inner giant. Be not mistaken; they too had their moments they had to grapple with and were determined enough to push through. They, too, had to do it scared at some point, whether it was daring to tame a lion, fight a fire-breathing dragon or tell someone they loved them for the first time. We've all been there. And we undoubtedly will be there again at some point.

All we need to survive and thrive in this life's journey is within us from the very start. Yes, we are each born with it. It does, however, take work to mine our inner caves so we can discover or rather uncover the treasure that has always been there. If we do the work of exploring the meanings behind our fears, such as asking when that fear began and charting it back to its inception, we can figure out if it is indeed our *own* fear or something that was imposed upon us by someone else, like family or friends. Then we can explore the possibility of what life would look like if that fear was nonexistent and ask ourselves how that fear is serving us in this particular instance. This is a great place to start. Because at a certain point if we are completely vulnerable and honest with ourselves in that work, our perspective will begin to shift. After being bullied and incarcerated by our fears, all of a sudden (but not really), one day we will wake up and sing a new tune. Perhaps it will start out as a slight hum, but it will be there, bubbling below the surface. When this happens, the questions become more charged: "What am I afraid of?" "If I do this thing, will I die if it doesn't pan out?" "Has anything I've ever done killed me before?" "If they can do it, why can't I?" "What makes them different?" "Who says I can't?" "They had never done it before they did it the first time, so what's the big deal?" Then finally the hidden questions are revealed because the mystique of fear is being illuminated and exposed. Which brings us to ask, "Can I?" "Can I have this thing?" "Can I do this thing?" "Can I achieve this thing?" "Can I be this thing?"

Finally, the answer comes in when we least expect it, and it's likely a quiet internal whisper that says, "Maybe I can!" And that, my friends, is the tiny glimmer of hope we need. A little bit of hope can go a long way on the road to loving ourselves beyond our fears. This is the "having the faith of the mustard seed" the Bible speaks of (Matthew 17:20, Luke 17:5-6). Once that momentum starts, the questions begin to turn a corner where our worth and confidence join the party. Fear switches from being the intimidator, to being intimidated. The looming shadow of the mountain that this fear once cast begins to fade in the sunlight as we step into our light and dance with destiny. Soon thereafter affirming statements become the self-talk we give airtime to. Statements like, "I've got this," "I've worked for this," "I deserve this."

This process, as painstaking as it can be, is different for each person. For some it might take a day; for others a month or even years. And then there are those who choose to never climb their mountains of fear—upon which there is no judgment. It's important to know, however, that fear coupled with our ego are intimate bedfellows that hold us separate from experiencing some of the truest parts of ourselves. The ego's insatiable appetite is nourished by our fears, which we in turn become slaves to if we aren't careful and aware. In essence our greatest lives are lived beyond the mountains of fear we falsely idolize.

I experienced this very thing once. I was growing tired of my budding casting career following my big move to Los Angeles. I'd been working on *America's Next Top Model* for a few years with very little deviation. And to be clear, upon my arrival in LA I'd fully thrust myself into the world of freelance. For those of you who don't know, the land of freelance is a wilderness of its own. It truly is a career of faith where you literally eat what you kill. And guess what, if you aren't working, you are not eating. I had no idea how difficult this choice would be, nor did I understand the great discipline it would require for me to survive in this jungle. With no mentor to help guide me along my path, I literally just made choices that felt good and made sense at the time.

After a few years, I'd mastered the casting realm and was itching to do more. My dilemma once again became whether I should stay where I was comfortable, well liked and respected, or move forward toward something more. Well I wouldn't make the same mistake of staying in a place that I had outgrown. Early on, right when I began to feel the boredom creep upon me, I asked a trusted friend and industry professional for some advice. I casually mentioned in conversation that I thought I might want to be a producer. Casting was fun, but I wanted to dig into the storytelling part more. To say it aloud for the first time was so exhilarating. Unfortunately, my exuberance was met with discouragement. This lovely person whom I'd had so much love and respect for said that it wasn't a good idea. They, too, had tried their hand in the producing arena, and they hated it, so much so that they discouraged me from even trying to venture down that road. They suggested that I stick with casting because I had a natural knack for it. I was completely crushed. Even though this individual wasn't officially my mentor (something they were uncomfortable committing to), I looked up to them as such. So, to hear my excitement met with anything less than encouraging words made me question myself. Was I being too ambitious? Was I thinking more of myself than I ought to? Could I, a young woman from the Bay Area who had no life plan or help from anyone actually dream bigger? Could I do and be more? Could I create my own path to success?

Well in this person's eyes in that moment, they were telling me to play it safe—like they had done. It took months for this chapter of my career to come to a close, but eventually it did. There came a moment when I had to realize that sometimes the people we love, as well-meaning as they are, cannot speak to what they have not had the courage to live themselves. This person wanted to produce at some point as well, but at their first try they got overwhelmed and discouraged and went back to what felt safe to them. I, on the other hand, came from an environment that didn't give me the room to quit. If I ever attempted to quit then I'd be quitting on myself, and I was all that I'd ever really had. Growing up, if I didn't push myself, no one else would. So, I learned early on that my only competition was me, and I always had to bet on myself. I felt like I was all I really had.

The day that I decided to bet on me and walk away from what I knew toward the unknown was troublesome for me. I prayed, paced, cried and called my god-brother, who asked me one simple question that made it click into place for me. He said, "So I hear you saying you want to be producer, but you have this casting job on the table and if you don't take it, you don't know if you'll have any work." I replied, sobbing, "Yes, that's correct." And he said calmly, "So what are you afraid of?" As a woman of faith, I knew that God had me, but I wasn't sure if I was being crazy or too ambitious. Who turns down good money and a solid job anyway? Who did I think I was? There were people lining up for this job, but here I was contemplating walking away. He encouraged me, and I took another huge leap of faith.

It would be eight long, trying months before I'd land my first producing gig. In this scenario I allowed the fears of someone else to permeate my very being. It caused me to doubt myself and the dream that was brewing in my heart. There was no malicious intent from that person, but I couldn't run her race and she couldn't run mine. Fast forward, here I am ten years later executive producing. Yes, there were times of famine and disappointment, but I'd rather be stressed while doing what I love than be miserable and doing what doesn't make my heart sing. The lesson is to never allow the fears of others to rob you of your destiny. I don't care if it's a friend, lover, parent, child, teacher, etc. Move through that projected fear and allow your heart to sing.

DOING IT SCARED

Take some time to list any fears that have been adopted by you or imposed upon you. It could be something big or small. For me it was my mother's fear of swimming that hindered me from wanting to learn to swim—something that I've begun to release as an adult. What fears have you picked up along the way? Maybe it's a fear of success? The Bible's scripture that speaks to the probability of a rich man making it into the kingdom of heaven is often misconstrued, but it's something that we are taught in African American communities. Whatever your fear might be, take a moment to write it down and really look at it. Is it yours? Or someone else's? Are there any steps you'd like to consider taking to move beyond the beliefs you've adopted? In the end my hope is that you come to the realization that the fear doesn't belong to you and it only has as much power as you give it. Consider putting it down and looking at the circumstance from another angle. Are you really afraid, or in acceptance and allowance of the fear at this point? How hard would it be to make a different choice? Remember, you have permission and you are allowed.

TAKEAWAYS:

- Love is the antidote for fear.
- A little bit of hope can go a long way on the road to loving ourselves beyond our fears.
- Fear and our ego are intimate bedfellows that keep us from experiencing some of the truest parts of ourselves.
- Never allow the fears of others to rob you of your destiny.

CHAPTER FIVE

DOING IT SCARED BECAUSE

WHAT'S FOR YOU ...IS YOURS

So far, we've covered a lot as we peel away the many masks of fear. I pray that you are feeling a little less intimidated by your situation, whatever it may be. Again, we are on this journey together, and being patient with ourselves is key throughout this process.

My pathway after Patchwerk took a few unexpected turns that eventually landed me in Los Angeles a couple of years later. But prior to that while still

Atlanta, taking jobs as a production assistant that paid a fraction of my previous salary was my source of survival. Beyond that, faith is what nourished me. It was such a humbling time because I discovered who my real friends and supporters were. I came to see that when the gloss that my job had provided for so many years began to fade, so did many friendships. My character was stripped, tested and rebuilt. In the midst of it I couldn't tell what God was doing in me, but there was definitely a crushing or refining that was occurring over the course of a few years. That span of time really was reminiscent of one of my favorite stories of the Bible—of Joseph and his colorful coat (Genesis 37). I learned first-hand that those who are meant to be by your side will stand with you at your bleakest moments and then celebrate with you when the win comes. And trust me, the win *always* comes . . . eventually.

I was largely alone during this period and focused on opening myself up to allowing my destiny to pull me forward. I had nothing to lose at this point anyway. Although I was making a tiny fraction of my previous salary, I never felt more alive and impassioned about anything. Working in production and behind the camera fed a part of me that I didn't know existed. It's like I was born to do it. My dying thirst had been quenched, and I practically worked for free with no complaints because it gave me life.

I remember one of my very first jobs as a PA (production assistant). It was on the music video set for "My Goodies" with Ciara featuring Petey Pablo. I was sure to arrive bright and early, fifteen minutes early, in fact. My call time was 7:00 a.m., and I didn't leave that video set until 10:00 a.m. the next day. After working for twenty-seven hours straight and being paid $150, beyond exhaustion, I felt invigorated because I was learning something new. The day was beyond long, and I have to say that it was one of the most humbling experiences for me because here I was picking up trash, fetching waters and ordering food for the very people who'd been my clients at the studio where I'd previously worked. My ego wanted to run and hide when I saw those same people witnessing me in a new "lower" position. I did all I could to hold my head high, but it ate away at me because I was accustomed to being on the other side of that elusive velvet rope. It can be rough when life seems to knock you down a peg, and not for some crime you've committed but just for growth's sake.

However, I was intrigued by this new adventure because even though I'd gotten my college degree, I'd never had practical, hands-on experience like this. Knowing that there was so much for me to learn ignited a fire in me that still burns today. It was that same passion I remembered feeling when I started that day at LaFace Records nearly ten years earlier. I was scared because I didn't know much about this television arena, but I knew how to work hard—and that's what got me through.

After spending a season of doing freelance PA work, I landed a job working with the now infamous Tyler Perry as his executive assistant. Ironically, I didn't know who Tyler was when I was told by well-known photographer Ernest Washington that he was looking for an assistant. Still figuring out what I wanted to do, I was open to any opportunity in media that would advance me, so I went in for an interview. On my second interview is when I actually met Tyler, who was so endearing yet slightly intimidating. He was self-made with his stage plays prior to Hollywood knocking at his door, so I was intrigued by his ambition, to say the least. During that meeting I spoke about my experience in the music business and how I'd recently decided to veer more toward television and film. I shared that I was a spiritual, God-fearing woman who was a Virgo. Anyone who knows a Virgo knows that we as a zodiac love each other, so that alone was a natural icebreaker. He too being a Virgo, we were able to create a natural synergy.

Walking away from that interview I wasn't sure what to expect, but I was hopeful because the interview had gone so well. The very next day I got the call that Tyler wanted to offer me the position to be his assistant. Simultaneously, an actor/producer friend of mine, Cedric, had also offered me a part-time job with him, as he was building his company at the time and had some intriguing projects on his plate.

Unsure of what I wanted, I unplugged and stepped away to PA on a gig out of town in the Bahamas for the weekend with friends who were event planners (now known as Verbal Slick). While on that trip I was in heavy meditation and prayer during my downtime about what lay ahead for me.

Tyler's offer was at face value a no-brainer opportunity, more stability, benefits and a solid and steady paycheck. The other offer didn't measure up comparatively, but there was room for me to expand and potentially produce, which was alluring even though I had no idea what it entailed. And I'd be working alongside a trusted friend.

The night before I returned home, I had a vivid dream that I was working on a movie set with my producer friend Cedric and we were in the thick of production. Waking up from that dream, I felt that I'd gotten confirmation of what my next move would be.

Here is where the fear set in for me. How could I willingly walk away from a job that would provide me the kind of stability I'd been searching for over an eight-month period? How would I tell this budding mogul that I'd rather take another offer over his? Was I completely crazy? But the thing was, my ambition had been awakened. At the time, the mere thought of possibly producing something (even though I had everything to learn about what that meant) was more attractive to me. And more than anything else, I felt like God was leading me toward taking a leap of faith over accepting the obvious choice. I learned amid this fear that money was not my motivation, but growth and fulfillment were. I cried at this realization because I recognized that I could be totally wrong in my choice. I could be walking past the very door that God was opening for me, and that was terrifying. But I had to follow my heart and trust that the God within me would not forsake me.

Once I returned home, the call from Tyler's office came, as they were eager for me to start my new job with them. Fear-FULL-y I politely declined the offer and said that I appreciated the opportunity. Still unsure of my decision, I'd done it scared. Moments later my phone rang, and it was Tyler himself asking why I'd declined the job.

Stunned, I was honest and told him that I'd prayed about it and gotten confirmation that I was to go in another direction. Taken aback, he said, "Well I prayed about it too, and God told me that you belong here working with me." We respectfully agreed to disagree, and I proceeded to take the other offer.

The summer was long and hot in Atlanta, and I was

busy holding down the fort with my producer friend in hopes that the dream I'd had would unfold sooner than later. Unfortunately, after only a few months of working with my friend, project funds were depleted, and he could no longer afford to pay me. Fear loomed yet again. How could I have been so wrong? I was frustrated and felt foolish for taking that leap of faith and turning down a solid opportunity.

Again, with nothing left to lose and my pride on the shelf, I called up Tyler's company to let them know that I was available again. It was unlikely that they'd even consider me after I declined their previous offer. But hours later, his VP called and said that if I still wanted the assistant position, it was mine. Apparently, after I declined the job offer, Tyler didn't want to hire anyone else, so the spot was still vacant. I was floored. Ultimately, that position was mine even though I'd walked away from it. It was held for me, for months!

So, when I hear someone say, "What's for you is for you," I believe it wholeheartedly because I lived it. And Tyler was actually right. Maybe God did indeed tell him that I belonged there, but I had to follow my heart and explore the other option. Tyler's offer came with all the bells and whistles and more money than my friend was offering, but again, money has never motivated me. I've found that following my purpose and what feels right to me always eventually pays out more dividends in the end.

DOING IT SCARED

Fear can cause us to believe that our situation is only as good as what is in front of our faces—what's tangible. We are misled in thinking that we can make a wrong choice when faced with a dilemma—red pill or blue pill?—when in all honesty, either scenario would actually present a plethora of lessons and opportunities for growth.

We can't be afraid to make the tough or unpopular choice for ourselves. We must challenge ourselves to put on courage and walk boldly toward what is calling us. In my case I did just that and received the benefit of both opportunities. In the end, I didn't lose at all—I WON! I won because **fearfully**, I chased my dream, and it indirectly led me back to a place that I belonged for a season. What dilemma are you currently facing? Perhaps it's a career change? Or maybe a relocation? No matter the dilemma, merely consider the option that brings joy to your heart at the very thought of it. Take a moment to travel there. With your imagination, explore your surroundings. How does it look, feel, and smell to be in that space? Who else is there with you? What is the energy like? What do you see? Be as detailed as you can. Live there for a moment, in that time and space.

That, my friends, is creation at its finest. The purpose of this practice is to show that we can literally create beyond the mountain of our fears. It is literally a reprogramming of how we see ourselves in a particular situation. Starting at this level of creation slowly chips away at fear's intimidating hold and allows us a glimpse beyond it. As our courage grows, fear seems to evaporate, allowing us the freedom to expand into our innate greatness.

In the end, no matter what we choose, destiny joins

us on that path and carries us forward. In other words, we can't get it wrong as long as we are following what feels good and right to us. And ultimately, as long as we live, there will always be another opportunity to choose again.

TAKEAWAYS:

- What is for you is YOURS. No one can change that. There is no "right" road.
- There are various paths that can lead to your happy ending.
- As courage is ignited, fear begins to evaporate, allowing us to expand into our innate greatness.

CHAPTER SIX

DOING IT SCARED

VULNERABILTY -OUR SOUL IN FULL BLOOM

In a previous chapter I mentioned love being the antidote for fear. But what if the fear that's being experienced is centered around the subject of love itself—being loved, being in love or loving another person? Fear is one of the most common emotions that bubbles to the surface when faced with love, whether it be on behalf of the giver, the recipient or both. Have you ever wondered why that is?

One theory I have is that in order to truly love, there must be a level of vulnerability that we are willing to surrender to. The problem here is, to truly be vulnerable we run the risk of being hurt, embarrassed and rejected. Considering that, there is no wonder fear creeps in. It takes guts and courage to be truly vulnerable, to let someone in, to be emotionally naked and exposed. Essentially the equation would be

something like this: vulnerability + courage to conquer fear = journeying toward the love we want. I believe that love is the answer to a multitude of problems and issues we experience in this life. The Bible speaks of love covering a multitude of sins (1 Peter 4:8). Unfortunately, we often search for love in the places that are not capable of yielding to us what we need.

Vulnerability is beautiful in that it is our authentic

self, radiating and projecting our truth to the world in a moment. When we're vulnerable, we share a glimpse of our heart and spirit with those around us. It's quite remarkable when you think about it. However, our willingness to be vulnerable threatens our ego. The ego is a very tricky part of our identity that if left unchecked will ruin relationships, opportunities and lives. It's our self-image and not a true representation of who we are. The ego, in all of its might, never recedes without a fight. It will fool us into unhealthy behaviors and then blame us when we self-destruct. In fact, the ego and fear are interdependent of one another, fooling us into false beliefs and leading us away from true self-awareness. Conversely, vulnerability forces a quiet humility within that encourages us to bear our souls and lead with love. It empowers us to create and face our fears no matter what the outcome might be.

Again, in *The Wizard of Oz,* those beloved characters had to put on the cape of courage to face their individual fears. At the onset of the story, their egos ruled their existence. They were falsely confident, bold and brave. But as they continued on the journey, the truth of who they really were was revealed while on that yellow brick road. They were wounded and afraid, each of them for various reasons. Their vulnerability with each other, where they shared their personal truths, is where the breakthroughs happened for each of them. They had to be authentic and expose their souls (vulnerability), which illuminated the path before them to face and conquer their fears. Once they did that, they were able to receive the love and acceptance from one another they'd desired from the onset.

SELF-LOVE

I believe that to experience healthy, balanced and satisfying love, we must first love ourselves. But how does one go about doing that? The term *love* itself is so loaded and can vary from person to person. *Self-love*, by definition, is having regard for one's own happiness and well-being. Allow that to sink in for a moment. I like to add to that statement the suffix of "above all others." So, it now reads, "having regard for one's own happiness and well-being above all others." This may seem selfish, but I argue that we cannot bless others with that which we don't possess.

From an early age we are instructed and taught that placing the happiness of another's above our own is proper and just. We unknowingly silence our "selfish ways" in the face of those we love in hopes they will fill us up, validate us or make us whole.

Over time we come to find that doesn't work. We eventually discover that no other person is responsible for or better yet even capable of making us happy— no matter how we slice it. It may seem for a short period that they make us happy, but in reality, they are a manifestation of how we feel about ourselves when in their presence. It's a very different concept.

Happiness is a personal inside job that demonstrates we are in alignment with ourselves and our inner being or God. As individuals, our wholeness is solely up to us. Placing our happiness, joy or bliss in the hands of another is a slippery slope that ends in disappointment every time. The reason is that people can only truly see a situation through the lens of their own experiences and disposition. Not to mention, no person (including you and me) can lend their undivided attention on one person or thing until infinity. It's unrealistic and unnatural. That's not to say that we can't empathize with and love one another, because we absolutely can.

The point is, we cannot expect another person to make us so important to them that our happiness rests solely upon them. We will be let down every single time. Every. Single. Time. Nobody wants that kind of responsibility—I sure don't. But how many relationships have you been in where this was your nonverbal expectation? Before I had this revelation, I was clearly in a fantasy world where I expected my partner to carry the load of my happiness. Today, if my partner were to say to me (and he never would say this), "I need you to be responsible for my happiness, and when I'm down you've gotta bring me back up because I can't do it alone," I'd run for the hills! I'm not capable of that job. I have too much in my own life that I'm concerned with and inspired by. As incredibly wonderful as he might be, I can't make a promise like that. It's too much pressure, and I'm bound to disappoint him on any given day.

I had to learn that my happiness is my own and that he is an extension of that emotion. He literally mirrors back to me where I am. We share in many happy moments together, for which I'm thankful, but when I'm in an unsavory mood, I admit it and dismiss myself to get back into a good vibration. Once I'm in a better place, then I rejoin him and we carry on. He does himself (and me) the same courtesy when he's in crappy mood. It reminds me of when riding an airplane; the flight attendant always instructs that in the event of a crash landing, we put on our own masks first, then assist our neighbors. Loving, honoring and prioritizing ourselves is key in being and attaining the love we say we want.

Of course, once we find a suitable partner, their needs and wants ought to have importance, and that's where compromising comes in. However, as we learn and grow, we come to find that pleasing others ought to come second to prioritizing ourselves and our own happiness. The thing is, oftentimes when we meet a special someone, we are swept away and get so enamored that we lose sight of ourselves. I honestly think that is the biggest challenge in loving relationships: not getting lost in or absorbed by our partners. I think we have all been there at some point and then come to resent our mates for allowing us to be eclipsed by them. Without judgment, as a woman, I tend to believe that we as a gender are more susceptible to this than our male counterparts. I've had many conversations with girlfriends over the years who willingly forfeited their individual identities and silenced their voices in exchange for a relationship, only to one day awaken from an internal slumber and not remember how they got to this particular place with their partner. I, too, have done this, so I can relate. I can't speak for them, but in my case, fear was largely the reason I ended up in those undesirable circumstances. Fear of being hurt, broken-hearted and abandoned—hauntings of my childhood trauma. A firm believer in the law of attraction, I respect that it is powerful at all times whether I choose to subscribe to it or not. In retrospect, the guys that I "fell for" were all a direct reflection of who I was on my journey at any given moment.

In one case in particular, I'd been living in Los Angeles for a few years when I met a really cool human being who I was instantly drawn to. Looking back, I think I was into him because at the onset he was into me—or at least that was the vibe I was getting. It's important to say that prior to this, work had been my focus. After relocating from Atlanta and starting a whole new career, men were not at all a priority for me. I was too busy concerning myself with survival to be focused on a man. However, when I met this one guy, I was a smitten kitten.

For the first several weeks, we spoke, emailed and texted constantly, and like an addict, I was hooked in no time. So, when the inevitable happened I began to freak internally. Why wasn't he calling as often? Or texting? For weeks it was like we were so absorbed in one another. Then, poof, magically he was over me? It didn't make sense and I didn't get it. More than that I couldn't or rather wouldn't accept it. Weeks turned to months that turned to years of me trying to get from him the same interest, excitement, and connection we initially had with each other. My friends coined him my "Mr. Big" after Carrie's elusive love interest in *Sex and the*

City. They couldn't understand why I was so into someone who seemingly overlooked me. They, as my friends, saw me as this empowered and confident woman and couldn't understand why I was wasting my time on a person who clearly didn't want me in a romantic way. I, on the other hand, was convinced that they all were wrong, and it was my mission to prove it to them.

I now realize that this was my fear and ego in the driver's seat driving like a crazed maniac leading me nowhere. Within fear's grasp I made one unhealthy decision after another. For years I was afraid to move on, in fear that I wouldn't meet anyone I connected with like him. And how could I trust that the next guy wouldn't pull back in the same way? I was questioning myself and trying to analyze whether I'd done something wrong. I was at the foot of a fear mountain. I refused to even address this mountain for years. I was afraid of so many things. I was afraid that I'd wasted so much time already. I was afraid that everyone else was right and I was wrong about us. I was afraid to be vulnerable and ask for what I really wanted. I was afraid to accept that his uncertainty about us was the truth. Him saying, "I don't know," in reference to us having a future was actually a hard "No". This was something I refused to accept for a long time, out of fear. I had basically been "friend-zoned." Accepting that meant that I couldn't trust my own instincts, and that's a scary place to be. I'll say it's important to note that neither me nor this unsuspecting gentleman did anything wrong. We were two people who wanted opposing things at the time— there's nothing wrong with that. Yes, I loved him, but I loved me more, and my relationship with myself was the most precious of them all.

The time finally came where I was courageous enough to bare my soul and ask for what I truly wanted: a committed romantic relationship. Admitting that to myself was a feat all in itself. I had to learn a big lesson about personal integrity during this time. Until we can be honest with ourselves, we are living a farce, and it was time for me to face the music. At the end of the day he didn't want the same things I did. A true relationship involves two willing participants, and we can't force anyone to be with us. I came to respect and accept his choice, something he'd been expressing all along. Once I acknowledged and accepted that his rejection meant redirection, I was fine to walk away. I realized that I was blocking the love that I was seeking by allowing so much of my emotional real estate to be occupied by this person. With an incredible support system of family and friends at my back, I came to realize that his choice had no reflection upon me. It was time for me to move on and see what was on the other side of this mountain. After all, it had to be better than what I had at the time. Once I let go of my expectation of more, a real, more balanced friendship was allowed to flourish, and for that I'm grateful.

I went on to find the love of my life a year later, and I'm thankful to all that I learned in that previous experience. The mountain of fear that walking away from that (non) relationship represented had a bounty of blessings awaiting me on the other side. My current love is everything I ever desired and everything I never knew I wanted in a partner. He is my hero, keeper of my secrets and guardian of my heart. He is the best man I know. I feel accepted and embraced, flaws and all. As we grow together, I've learned to make it a point to purposefully be vulnerable with him because through those cracks is where the love flows in, and love is everything.

The biggest difference between these two relationships is how I showed up. Although I've always been an advocate for self-love, growth, and introspection, the above experience threw me for a loop. Along the way I lost sight of me and directed focus to someone else—in hopes they would fill me up in the same ways I'd grown accustomed to. It was an unrealistic and unfair expectation to place upon that man.

Essentially, the response that I was getting from him was reflecting how I felt about myself deep down in that interaction. Until I saw myself more highly and felt deserving and worthy of more, I was stuck in the loop of that lesson. But once I got it, it was over. Later, I recognized that my self-love meter must have been idling low, so low, in fact, that I'd lost clear sight of me and what I deserved. Until I was courageous enough to be honest with myself, I wore any and every mask that I needed to protect me from facing the truth of my situation. I was finally able to understand that real transparency is transformative. I awakened to the fact that I am worthy of love. I don't have to earn love. I'm worthy simply because I breathe. I'm worthy because God wakes me up daily in my right mind, and if that isn't an expression of infinite love, I don't know what is. I give thanks for it all, for it made me a better and more evolved version of myself.

DOING IT SCARED

In the above scenario I stalled on facing a fear even though I was unfulfilled. Fear showed up in new and clever ways for me in that relationship. I hid behind pride, spirituality, stubbornness, the fact that I'm a giver, and unworthiness all in an effort to avoid facing my fear of rejection. I didn't want to be heartbroken, and I stacked the deck against myself because I refused to be honest. I held on for dear life to something that no longer served me because I refused to be wrong. I had to softly love myself through those revelations and exercise patience when reconnecting with inner magic. I came to know that all the love we need in this life we have been born with. God grants us that right at our very first breath. Every question that arises, we have the power to answer when we are still and quiet. After allowing my heart to break over that relationship, I decided I wanted to create my next relationship. If nothing else, I wanted to be the best version of myself before I met my Mr. Right. I began a ritual of daily meditation aside from praying so that I could visualize myself in my mind's eye. I believe we truly are as we see ourselves.

Over time I began to feel myself becoming whole and happy. There was no particular reason other than I convinced myself that I deserved to be satisfied no matter what my circumstance was. Happiness is free, and it's a conscious choice. Life, of course, happens, but it's all in how we choose to see things. I for one have always seen the glass as half full—the eternal optimist.

One day I was inspired to write a list on a Post-it note of how I wanted to feel in my new relationship. It was an odd thought, but I went with it.

I wrote at the top of the Post-it, "In my new relationship I feel . . ." I then proceeded to imagine myself on the happiest day in my fantasy relationship. It was a culmination of every corny movie, play, and R&B song I'd ever experienced all rolled into one. I listed over fifty emotions that I felt while in this trance. A few that I wrote were as follows: safe, sure, accepted, secure, considered, loved, appreciated, happy, giddy, sexy, understood, accepted, naughty, free, uplifted, liberated, supported, lighthearted, fun, funny, friended, powerful, allied, harmonious, and vulnerable. The list went on for as long as I could come up with descriptive feeling words.

After writing it, I folded it and then tucked it away in my wallet and forgot all about it. I carried it in my wallet for months, and sometimes when I would come across it, I'd pull it out, read it aloud then go on about my day. I didn't talk to anyone about it, as it was baking in the oven, so to speak. You never want to disrupt that process.

God had it under control. I didn't compare the list to any of the guys that I was entertaining at the time. I allowed it to live in the ethos, as my only work was to attract it. The list was my work. The rest was up to God and the universe.

You'll notice I wrote nothing about his looks, his occupation or his status. I focused only on how I would feel in a relationship with this unknown king of mine. About eight months later, playing around online, I came across an email from the man I'm now with. Go figure!

I've rewritten that Post-it several times over while in my relationship as we continue to grow together—as it's always about maintenance. Yes, I had attracted him, but I won't lie and say that at the time I felt every emotion on that list, because I didn't initially. We had to learn about each other and grow together. But I do today, years into the relationship.

When we have our ups and downs, I revisit the list, sit in mediation and create a new one—never discarding the old ones, as I like to be a witness to our journey together.

Since that time, I've written Post-its for jobs, friendships and other experiences with the intention to create my world as I'd like it to be. It really is quite magical when we put pen to paper with purpose. I promise you it works. One of the key components is to release the resistance around the subject—lay it on paper then walk away from it. When we are able to release the resistance we are then open, to allowing the thing we want to come into our experience.

Your turn! My friend, I challenge you to take a subject that is important to you and create it on a Post-it like the example above. Create the experience in your mind as you'd like it to be. A

Post-it is tiny and nonthreatening, so it's an ideal place to start. Whether it be for a job, a move, starting a business, buying a house, a broken friendship, a relationship or an opportunity—it can be for any and everything. Give it a try. It may feel weird at first, as it will force you to completely ignore reality, but that's okay for a spell. You have permission. This is faith at work, the mustard seed that the Bible speaks of (Matthew 17:20, Luke 17:5-6). Center yourself and imagine what it feels like to be living in that specific situation if it were absolutely perfect. Take your time with it. Don't rush through the process.

It's important to use feeling or emotional words only, not phrases. You don't want to include anything that you don't want on the list. In this creative space you can have it exactly the way you want it, so don't be afraid to ask and dream. Really allow yourself to feel each emotion as the word bubbles up and surfaces in your mind. You will be tempted to use phrases and talk about what you don't want, and I encourage you away from that. Try your best to focus on singular feeling words that describe an emotion.

In the end, if your list only produces ten words, that's perfectly fine. You can always add to and expand the list later if you choose. The point is not to judge but to open yourself up to the possibility of something perfectly crafted just for you. Good luck, and cheers to creating something magnificent.

TAKEAWAYS:

• Vulnerability illuminates our path toward love. To be vulnerable is to be human. • Our willingness to be vulnerable threatens our ego and forces a quiet humility within that says, "No matter what the outcome might be, this thing, I must do, say or be."

• No other person is responsible or, better yet, even capable of making us happy. That is our job alone.

• We are each worthy of love simply because we breathe.

• We ought not be afraid to ask for what we want in a loving relationship. It's our right.

• We have the power to create our life experiences. What are you creating?

• It's okay to love someone, but we must

love ourselves *more*.

- True transparency from within is transformative.

CHAPTER SEVEN

DO IT SCARED BECAUSE

YOU'VE ALREADY BEEN VALIDATED

One of the most challenging aspects of being human is our desire for approval and validation from others. From the careers we pursue, to the cars we drive and the clothes we wear, we are often secretly in search of some sort of approval or acknowledgement—validation. It's not something that we willingly admit, but essentially, it's true for most of us. Let's be honest; no one wants to be or feel invisible. The danger arises when we begin to rely upon the praise of others to feed our self-esteem and image.

With the awesome advent of technologies such as social media, this becomes a very slippery slope. We inadvertently adopt addictions that aren't necessarily beneficial to our self-image. Not many addictions are. Constantly having cosigners to affirm a perceived version of us can take its toll over time. As mere humans we are all susceptible to handing over the keys of our lives to the ego, who will eventually drive us off a cliff and blame us for the carnage. Constant attention from being seduced by affirming comments, likes and heart-eyed emojis has the power to suck us into a vortex and overtake us. As a practice in self-discipline, I purposefully take breaks from social media from time to time to ensure a healthy internal balance as well as to dismiss myself from the opinion and validation of others.

It's taken a good deal of lumps, bumps and self-work to get to where I am internally. My life is just now beginning to reflect the harvest of what was seeded and attended to over time—lots of time. However, for a while because of my childhood trauma, I was fearful that I'd never be enough and was convinced that the "things" that I cloaked myself with legitimized me in some way. Those things provided me with a false sense of security, and the mere thought of being without them was daunting. I'm sure you've met someone who, when you were introduced, told you what they did instead of who they were. We can become so engulfed in what we have and do that it's difficult to ascertain where the "things" end and "we" begin. It may sound something like, "Hi, I'm Erika, an executive producer," instead of, "Hi, I'm Erika, a caring person of great integrity who wants to inspire others to be great and win."

Here in Hollywood and in the entertainment business especially, the former is the most common. The notion that what I did for a living or what I possessed defined me was a mental construct. I had to reprogram my mind after a series of life events that revealed to me that we are ever moving and expanding—so holding fast to our sense of self is our true north. As long as the North is steady, we can adapt to the rest.

For me, growing up in the inner city definitely had an impact on how I view the world in which I live. By nature, I'm a kind, generous and compassionate person at heart. By nurture, on the other hand, I'm an around-the-way ride-or-die girl with slightly hood tendencies, who often roots for the bad guys in movies. I can't explain it, but it's true. My father and uncles were all street dudes who gifted me with common sense and hipped me to the "game of life," so to speak. I saw a lot of things no young girl should ever see, but now that I'm an adult, not much shakes me to my core. So, I count it all joy. To the naked eye I present as polished, but not many know my story, as it's not something I lead with. It is always there, however, resting on my shoulder, reminding me of where I came from.

No different from anyone else, acceptance is something that is important to us all. We as humans value the acceptance of others whether it be family, friends or fans. We unconsciously adjust to our surroundings and to others in hopes that we will be accepted and embraced by them. For instance, being a Black woman in Hollywood, I've had to contort myself into a palatable nonthreatening representation to be accepted and embraced. Interestingly, for many years I was ashamed to admit that I was raised in a home where drugs were commonplace, and that my father abused my mother to the point of her abandoning my brother and me leaving him to raise us. My father was an amazing parent but unfortunately not the best partner to my mom at the time. I'm thankful that today they are both clean, healthy and maintain a respectful friendship with one another. They honestly did they best that they could with parenting my brother and I – so I hold no ill feelings nor judgement toward either of them. In fact, I if given the chance to choose my parents again (from the spirit realm) I'd make the same choice twice over because I would not be who I am today without either of them – they are my heartbeat and I love them both dearly.

At any rate, I was so embarrassed and afraid of judgment in my earlier years, that I never shared what I was going through with anyone. Just like in most Black households, sharing family business was frowned upon.

Not even my best friend, who I was with every day since the age of twelve, was aware of my situation. I always played it cool, arrived to school on time, and was determined to make education my golden ticket to a different kind of life. It wasn't until we were away at college that I shared my truth with her. My fear was that nobody would understand and that somehow, I would be judged and looked down upon because my life was less than perfect. I thought I wouldn't be accepted and that I wasn't enough on some level. I was ashamed, not as result of my own behavior, but because of the choices and actions of others.

I had to come to a place of self-acceptance, love and courage to be vulnerable in front of my very best friend. In order to share with her what I thought might cause her to judge me and abandon me, I had to face the fear and dismiss the shame. It might sound ridiculous, but we do it all the time in our human experience. We write a script in our minds and then organize our lives to support that script even if it's something we don't want. We use our magic against ourselves instead of for ourselves. After sharing my secret with Lisa, I found that there was no way on earth she would have "unfriended" me for the reasons my fear had convinced me of. It's odd because when we are in the grips of fear, we are married to it, and it's quite comfortable—more so than the unknown. But once we are on the other side of fear, we can't understand why we were ever afraid in the first place. This, of course, was not the last occurrence of me operating in fear and shame, because we rarely get the lesson the first, second or third time around. I remember not sharing things of importance with friends because deep down I knew something was amiss. Have you been in that place? So ashamed to tell the whole truth that you share half-truths about a situation in order to avoid judgment? But in reality, you are judging yourself? I've come to realize that if I can't be totally transparent about what's going on, then I'm in a place of fear.

Living here in Los Angeles adjacent to Hollywood where everyone comes to fulfill a dream of making it big was intimidating initially. Especially being a woman of color in the entertainment business, I always knew that I'd have to play by a separate set of rules in the game. Frankly, the game could be looked at as a microcosm of society, where it's rigged against someone who looks like me—at least until recently. This meant that I had to be better than average. I still do. My work ethic had to be unmatched, and sleep became the enemy.

This mentality was not new to me. While in college at Clark Atlanta University and taking a full load of courses, I worked simultaneously at Patchwerk Recording Studios, La Face Records and Hitco music publishing under the late and always poppin' playboy Shakir Stewart, RIP. Juggling two jobs while going to school was no small feat, but failure was not an option. Not to mention, working in the presence of people like LA Reid, Billie Woodruff, Sharliss, Dallas, KP, DL Warfield, TLC, Usher, Taiye, Ludacris, TI, Dungeon Family, Ciara, Jazze Pha, B.Cox, J-Que, Eric Dawkins, Eric Cire, Pooh Bear, Scarface, Outkast, Lil Jon, Goodie Mob, J. Geter, 2 Chainz, Noontime, 112, Dru Hill, Destiny's Child, Kai Crawford, Chris Hicks, Lil Jon, KP, Jim Crow, Ian Burke, and Dilla Johnson (the list literally goes on) was like being amongst a class of greatness.

These were only some of the cool kids during that booming music era in Atlanta. It was inspiring not because of who they were at the time (because they were still striving and building), but because they refused to quit, and they carved a path for themselves. Today they are each legendary in their own right and I'm honored to have witnessed their greatness up close and in person.

When I was deciding to leave the casting portion of my career and launch into producing, it was scary, as I mentioned in a previous chapter. Initially I was excited about the possibility of what could be ahead. As time ticked on, I became weary. Unemployment insurance barely covered my monthly bills, and the properties that I still owned back in Atlanta were on the brink of foreclosure. Life got hard, and fear crept back in yet again. I began to question my decision to bet on myself by taking that leap of faith. I sent emails daily, applying to jobs for months on end. I grew angry and eventually depressed. As a woman of faith, I was determined not to let my situation break me—but one day in particular the anger became palpable. I was afraid to admit that I was mad at God. But how was I supposed to settle that? For weeks on end I did nothing; I sat on those feelings. Obviously, God knew my heart, so I was running from facing myself, but that was more comfortable than facing my truth at the time. Low and behold at the eighth-month mark, the anger that had been an undercurrent surfaced while I was in prayer. Something in me broke. I confronted God. I cried, I yelled, I pleaded and literally lost it. I couldn't understand why I was being punished for facing my fear and taking a leap of faith. I felt like God had indeed forsaken me.

I complained that I no longer had my job, my security, money, the title that I'd worked so hard for, a mate and so on. I questioned if I was even in the right field. In fact, if at that moment God had told me to go and be a bank teller, I would have. The "wilderness" had gotten to be too much to bear at this point. Bear in mind this was my third go at being in this kind of situation for an eight-month period, so I was beyond over it. I had been faithful, patient, obedient, strong and unwavering. I was empty, and honestly, I was embarrassed. I felt like a failure. Fear was kicking my ass. I was at the end of my rope, and I needed God to move and shake something loose in the heavens for me.

Have you ever been in this place? It's such a painful existence. I was on an island all by myself, and I wanted off. I wanted my life back, and if that meant starting over again, I was fine with it. Direction is what I was desiring.

Moments following my temper tantrum I lay on my bedroom floor in a puddle of tears quiet, staring above. And in that quiet I heard these words loud and clear, "None of that validates you . . . I validate you." Boom! When I tell you that I had gotten a word, that was a word for my life! None of that validated me. Not the man (or lack thereof), the job, the title, the car or any of it. None of that stuff mattered if those things had me and I was ruled by them. And by not having any of those things at the time, I had to acknowledge that I was actually okay. I was still healthy, breathing, walking, talking and in my right mind. None of those material or superficial things really mattered. My character, my integrity, and my heart being pure were what mattered. I was literally schooled in that moment and so thankful for it. I had to relinquish my need and want for control over the situation and allow it to just be. I had to release my resistance and therefore allow the good that God had in store to flow into my life.

Four days later, I got called in to interview for a job I'd applied for online. After a couple of intimidating interviews with that show, I ended up with a position higher than what I'd applied for *and* a raise. I was given beauty for my ashes.

The moral of the story is that you have already been validated. God validates you each day you awake with breath in your body. The extraneous influences and material frills are fluff. They are outside of you. They are not who you are. None of those "things" create us nor make us whole. Only we can do that by connecting with our God source, whatever that might be. It's important to consider who we are minus all of the attention, money, fame, material wealth, etc. that we have or are striving toward. Because those things, as great as they might be, also have the power to seduce us away from our innate virtue. Self-work, evaluation and taking the time to be introspective is the food that our soul craves. Be not afraid to venture within. Ultimately, we are destined to win. The game is rigged in our favor.

DOING IT SCARED

Have you ever had a wilderness experience? A time in your life where you've ventured out on your own with no direction and nothing but the wind at your back? I've had several wilderness experiences, and no matter how many times I've been there, it never seems to get any easier while in the midst of it. Of course, without fail fear always finds a way of creeping in and taking root at some point on that journey. And it's not until I face my fears that I'm awakened to my glorious tomorrow.

The following activity is something that I did nearly ten years ago, and it was so cathartic and powerful. It allowed me to encourage myself during a dark time, and I trust that it will do the same for you. Recounting pivotal moments in our lives can be an encouraging practice. So often we focus on the rough and difficult times and neglect the victories we've experienced.

I invite you to write a letter to your childhood self, from your adult stance today. Begin the letter as you would any other, addressing it to the youngest version of you that you can recall. Imagine being that small child and opening this letter that is essentially a voice from the future. What kind of encouragement, support and warnings will you lend? What types of advice will you share in hopes that the younger you might avoid pitfalls? How will you explain or prepare them for any pain that might be on the horizon? The goal is to be honest with your younger self with the feeling that he or she can overcome any and all of it. Remember, you are currently standing in your young self's future, which is your present, so the victory has been won thus far. That's the best news yet!

In my letter I warned little erika of the troublesome home life she'd experience but assured her that she'd eventually leave that nest and create a journey all her own. There is no right or wrong way to address this task, as we each have a different story and perspective. So please be gentle with yourself about it. In the end you will realize how many difficult mountains you have not only climbed but conquered. You'll witness that validation from anything outside of yourself in light of all this will pale in comparison to your overcoming. You've already been validated, dear heart. Embrace your greatness.

TAKEAWAYS:

- If we live by the validation of others – we also die by the criticism of others.

- You have already been validated – you were born into validation.

- It's important to consider who we are minus all of the attention, money, fame, material wealth, etc. that we have or are striving toward.

- If we refuse to venture within – we eventually go without.

CHAPTER EIGHT

DOING IT SCARED BECAUSE

WE JOURNEY TO FEAR

TO JOURNEY THROUGH FEAR

By now you will have come to a new place with regard to your fears since beginning this journey with me. I know I have! As we bring this spiritual expedition to a close, I want to gift you something—an inspiring charge, if you will. But before that let's cover one more area that has the potential to plague us all: fear of the unknown.

Have you ever been in a really unhealthy situation

and afraid to move past it, be it a job, relationship, friendship or otherwise? Or conversely, have you maybe been so comfortable in a situation that stepping out beyond felt too risky? We've all heard the adage, "If it isn't broke, then don't fix it." In other words, don't rock the boat that we've mastered the rhythm of. But shouldn't the point of being alive be to thrive?

Fear will convince us that where we currently stand is as good as it gets—and that's not necessarily true. Again, in this life that is constantly in motion, we must grow and evolve.

On the one hand, the unknown is exactly that: uncharted territory that can be more intimidating than intriguing, more spooky than inspiring. On the other hand, it can also be what has been referred to as the field of pure potentiality or infinite creativity, a place where we create the magic that is then manifested into our lives. It's a blank slate, if you will, awaiting us to color it into life. In the realm of the unknown there lie a multitude of opportunities for us to shock and delight ourselves beyond our wildest imaginations. When you think about it, our perspective is key. What if what resides beyond the mountain of the unknown isn't our worst fears realized, but rather every single joy that we have ever wanted? The promised land, if you will. What if we could allow ourselves to view the unknown from a nonjudgmental and compassionate place?

There are times that we can overthink a thing, causing us to remain stagnant. We put things off by procrastinating and filling our lives with distractions, busying ourselves so much that time passes us by. We analyze, debate and make lists of pros and cons, further prolonging taking any action. My brilliant partner calls it "paralysis by analysis." We procrastinate.

I know this to be true because I've done it. This book is a prime example of all of the above. For ten years this piece of work has been incubating, and I found every reason not to sit and just write. I wasn't ready. I wasn't sure. I wasn't positive that I would be good at nor able to complete it. I realize now that I was afraid. With each written page it became a little bit easier, a little less intimidating. The point is that the fear will never just go away all on its own. We can't wait it out, so to speak. That is not the nature of fear. It will remain. *We*, however, are charged to walk toward that mountain and step into that arena of the unknown to discover another powerful layer of ourselves. Personally, I've come to the point in life where I know if fear is present then I *must* lean into it and not run from it. I'm scared the whole time. Once I conquer that fear, I know that the probability of another fear being right around the corner is not just possible but probable.

But we must realize that we journey to fear so that we can journey *through* fear. We ought to be encouraged that in this process of becoming fear warriors and doing it scared, we are allowed to bear witness to our evolution. Success at its very best.

I don't have all of the answers, and my perspective is exactly that, my own. I'm thankful for your willingness to travel on this expedition with me. It was not easy, but here we are at the end. We've done it! My prayer is that you walk away from this book with more clarity on how worthy, amazing and powerful you are—and we are. We are all in this life thing together. So in light of that, consider reading the below aloud to yourself whenever you are confronted by fear, discouragement and self-doubt.

Fear is to be conquered even if you have to DO IT SCARED!

CHAPTER NINE

DOING IT SCARED BECAUSE YOU ARE COMPLETE

Have you any idea how magnificent you are? From the crown of your head to the soles of your feet, you are God's imagined perfection. You are unmistakably one of a kind. A standout. Like a fingerprint, there has never been and there will never be another you. This life journey that you've chosen to experience is yours for the making. Your mind is a wide-open field of imagination, and your words are your enchanting wand. You are powerful. You are magic. You deserve to win. You can manifest anything you want. Bliss your way into happiness. You are incredibly wonderful. You are loved. You are appreciated. You are powerful. You are strong and courageous. You are worthy. You are magical and so magnificent. You are perfectly designed by the divine. You are brilliant, and your mind is infinite with ideas and life-changing solutions. You are beautiful; the love of God radiates through your skin for the world to witness. You are love. You are loved. You are light. You are liked. You are important. You are built for this. You deserve to thrive and be happy. You are worthy. You are enough. You are special and so remarkably exquisite. Again, you are enough. You are ready. It is your time. It is your destined time. You are fearless. You have every answer you need. You can do anything you put your attention and focus on. You are exactly where you need to be. You are whole. And you are complete. You are a blessing. You are blessed.

Whatever has caused you to feel afraid, shy, reluctant, ashamed, fearful, bashful, discouraged, rejected, unworthy, small, less than or unequipped, DO IT SCARED! Build. Love, then love again. Begin a new thing. Pursue a dream. Start over. Leave. Travel. Be vulnerable. Start a business. Speak your truth. Bet on yourself. Buy that home. Or sell that home. Write that book. Create that masterpiece. Ask for that raise or promotion. Start meditating. Start working out. Commit to something. Get married. Start a family. Admit your faults. Be vulnerable. Write that song. Take that stage. Forgive that person. Ask for what you want. Use your voice. Be your true self. In essence, stretch yourself toward the sun on the other side of fear's mountain—more of life awaits you. And so it is. *Ase.*

Thank you!

I'd like to take a moment to thank you kindly for purchasing my book Doing It Scared. I realize you could have chosen any number of authors to support and you chose this path. If you enjoyed this book and have been inspired in some way by the words on these pages, I'd like to hear from you and hope you find time to post a review on Amazon. Also feel free to share this book with your family and friends by posting to Facebook, Instagram and Twitter. Please know your feedback and support are greatly appreciated. Wishing you the very best in life, love and happiness.

xoxo - eb

IG: ebryant22

erika-bryant.com

chapter8publishing@gmail.com

NOTES:

NOTES:

Made in the USA
Las Vegas, NV
27 March 2021

20310924R00100